MAKING HOLY THE DAY

MAKING HOLY THE DAY

A Commentary on the Liturgy of the Hours

by

CHARLES E. MILLER, C.M.

"By your gift I will utter praise
in the vast assembly. . . ." (Psalm 22:26)

CATHOLIC BOOK PUBLISHING CORP.
New Jersey

Imprimi Potest:

> Joseph S. Falanga, C.M.
> *Provincial, Los Angeles Province*

Nihil Obstat:

> Daniel V. Flynn, J.C.D.
> *Censor Librorum*

Imprimatur:

> ✠ James P. Mahoney, D.D.
> *Vicar General, Archdiocese of New York*

(T-410)

ISBN 978-0-89942-410-1

PREFACE

This little book is meant not only for priests, deacons, and religious but for all the faithful. It is clearly the mind of the Church, as expressed in the Constitution on the Sacred Liturgy (100), that every Catholic should view the Liturgy of the Hours as the prayer book of all the people of the Church, and not of a select few. Consequently this booklet is written in a simple, direct style so that all can derive benefit from it. It is not a rubrical book. One should come to it with some familiarity of "how to say" the Liturgy of the Hours, and preferably with a copy of that prayer book close at hand for easy reference. Also, reading this commentary is not a substitute for a close study of the General Instruction of the Liturgy of the Hours.

The author hopes that this presentation, besides being a personal guide toward making holy the day, can serve as a starter for discussions among priests with each other, as well as with their people, and among religious. It can also be used in seminary liturgy classes.

It is by God's gift that we "utter praise in the vast assembly" (Psalm 22:26). May all God's people joyfully and devoutly make use of this great gift.

Charles E. Miller, C.M.
St. John's Seminary
Camarillo, California

CONTENTS

PART I

GENERAL REFLECTIONS

Chapter 1
PRAYING THE CHURCH'S WAY

"The Spirit helps us in our weakness" (Romans 8:26).

When I was a child I prayed as a child. I said prayers I had memorized at home and in school. When I made my first communion I received a book with a white cover and lots of pictures and prayers composed by a priest whose name I have now forgotten. These experiences helped to shape my understanding of prayer at a time when I was most impressionable.

When I became a man, the Church asked me to put aside childish prayers as it placed in my hands another prayer book, then known as the Roman Breviary. The transition was not easy, not primarily because the book was in Latin (the year was 1955), but because the way of praying was so different from those deep-seated impressions of childhood. To begin with, most of my prayers had been those of petitions which were pretty much centered on my own welfare, both spiritual and physical, and now I found prayers (mainly Psalms) which reflected many varied human emotions beyond my own personal experience, and which with rather relentless consistency turned from attitudes of personal or community need to praise and worship of God. The Psalms, or better the divine author of the Psalms, cried out to me to grow beyond my own limited horizons and to look up to God not only as a source of help but as a Person deserving of my unending praise and thanks.

But I should not overdraw the picture. My training both as a seminarian and as a Vincentian prepared me well for the Divine Office and for its chief component, the Psalms. The point is that early impressions, however appropriate they may have been at the time, are not easily changed. The Office was at first a thrill. I was proud to be seen with my book, a sign that I was in major orders. All too soon the thrill wore off and the sign value was placed in a less self-conscious perspective. It was only by the grace of God contained in the Office itself that I made a step, however short, toward some kind of maturity in prayer. And that leads us to the real value of the Office, now better known as the Liturgy of the Hours.

The Holy Spirit's Work

The genius of the Church is that it has chosen as the chief component of its official prayer book the Psalms. The Psalms, it is true, grew out of human experiences both of individuals and of the community of Israel, but ultimately they are not man-made prayers as was the collection found in the book given me at my first Holy Communion. The Psalms are inspired prayers; they are the composition of the Holy Spirit. If I find the Psalms difficult or foreign to me, I must recognize that in the human condition I remain somewhat alienated from God —distant from him—despite the grace of Jesus Christ. In our human condition "we do not know how to pray as we ought" (Romans 8:26). Grace is at work in us, but its effect is not always instantaneous. We all need to grow in grace. And through the grace of Christ the gift of the Spirit is given us. "The Spirit . . . helps us in our weakness," praying within us (Romans 8:26f), and he helps us in limitless ways. One of those ways is by placing in our hands a book of inspired prayers. To these prayers we must come, not to find favorites suitable to our mentality, but in order to grow closer to the mind of God, to the way God wants us to pray.

The prayer book of the Church, besides containing inspired prayers, includes inspired readings. God speaks to us in those readings, and the Church has arranged the readings in such a way that together with those used in the Mass we cover virtually the entire content of both Testaments. Most people have favorite passages from scripture, and it is good for us to return again and again to those parts of the Bible which move us and fit our personal needs. And yet the Church wishes us to grow in our knowledge and love of *all* of God's word.

With faith we should see how beautiful this book called the Liturgy of the Hours really is: God speaks to us and we respond to him in words and sentiments he himself has inspired through the Spirit. To these words of God are added some words of the Church (such as the Intercessions) as the Spirit continues to help the Church in its weakness. These words, officially sanctioned by the Church, are more precious than those of any single human author.

Nothing then can adequately substitute for this prayer book of the Church. It is true that bishops and major religious superiors have the authority to commute the Office to some other form of prayer. Such commutation may be justified in individual cases and for a period of time, but the arrangement and content of the Office allow for and even occasion a spiritual development and maturity which cannot be found elsewhere. In addition the Office brings us into a unity of prayer with many brothers and sisters throughout the whole world.

Sanctification of the Day

The Constitution on the Liturgy set up principles which returned the Office to its original purpose, the sanctification of the day. We old-timers can remember when we lumped together several hours, such as all four Little Hours, or Matins with Lauds, or Vespers with Compline, in order "to get them out of the way." Worse still, we sometimes found ourselves around eleven at night trying to squeeze in the entire Office before midnight. With simplification and a reduction in the number of hours, the Church makes it possible and even convenient for us to pray the hours at the appropriate times. The wish of the Church is clearly that all Catholics should make use of this opportunity to make holy the entire day. One should not think that the office is principally monastic in character. The early Christians, long before monastic orders arose in the Church, were dedicated to the praying of the Psalms and the reading of God's word, originally a valuable heritage from Jewish practice. Although the office was later shaped and added to by monastic practice, the Church has now restored the office to a form of prayer suitable for all devout Catholics.

The plea that we are too busy in our modern world for the office reflects a confusion of values. We all make time for what we consider to be important. Nothing can be more important than the fact that "God chose us in Christ before the world began to be holy . . . and to praise his glory" (Ephesians 1:44f). And the posture that "my work is my prayer" is at best a misdirected zeal and at worst a weak rationalization. As we shall see in a later chapter, the office is truly an apostolic prayer, well suited to those engaged in an active ministry whether as a priest, religious, or lay person.

Morning Prayer (Lauds) and Evening Prayer (Vespers) are the chief hours, placed at those times most appropriate for prayer, namely, when the day is beginning and when the day is drawing to a close. Between these two extremities is placed Daytime Prayer, and just before retiring is Night Prayer (Compline). The Office of Readings may be celebrated at any convenient hour.

The Eucharist is the high point of every day, and is no longer limited to any particular time. The Eucharist is the focal point of all the hours of the office. Morning Prayer should always precede the Eucharist since as a prayer of praise it prepares for and leads to the Eucharist.

Evening Prayer is best prayed after the Eucharist and looks back to its celebration. Daytime Prayer is a reaffirmation of our dedication to God's work as expressed and deepened in the Eucharist. The Office of Readings is either a meditative preparation for Mass or a reflection upon it, depending on when it is prayed.

The Prayer of Christ

Most important of all is the fact that the Psalms are Christian prayer, not only because their meaning is fulfilled in Christ, but also because Jesus Christ prayed the Psalms. I like to reflect on these words of Psalm 17:

> Turn your ear to my prayer:
> no deceit is on my lips. . . .
> You test me and you find in me no wrong.
> My words are not sinful as are men's words.

Apparently the Psalmist had in mind a specific incident in which he had been falsely accused, but I am personally nonetheless reluctant to proclaim before God that he will find no wrong in me. There is a person who can say these words without qualification. That person is Jesus Christ. And say them Jesus did. This Psalm, in fact, tends to remind me that as a good Jew, Jesus prayed the Psalms. As Priest through the hypostatic union Jesus made the many sentiments of the Psalms his own and in praying them he expressed his union with all men which had come about by means of his incarnation. So, leaving aside the scriptural problem about the *ipsissima verba Christi* in the gospels, it is clear that the Psalms, in translation of course, are indeed the prayer of Jesus Christ.

That Jesus prayed the Psalms adds a new dimension to these inspired prayers. Praying them, I come into contact with Jesus Christ and through him with all the people of the world. During all liturgical prayer the union of Head and members takes on a dynamic, active quality, but the Psalms as the actual prayers of Jesus on this earth have a special meaning and flavor. I have never been to the Holy Land. I would like to see the terrain where Jesus walked with his disciples, where he worked his miracles, and where he died and rose. But within the prayer book of the Church I have something more precious—the very Psalms Jesus prayed.

I am convinced that Jesus Christ wants to continue these prayers through the members of his Church. I believe that he still wants to make their sentiments his own, as through us he unites himself with every man. Personally when I feel a little bored with the Office or think that I am too busy or too tired for it, I try to open my ears to hear Jesus saying to me, "Let me pray the Psalms today through you. Help me pray in the person of all my people." Using the prayer book of the Church in union with Jesus Christ, we can indeed make holy the day.

Chapter 2
CELEBRATION

"Where two or three are gathered together . . ."
(Matthew 18:20).

In another generation when people saw a cassocked priest walking slowly around the church yard with a black book in his hand, they knew that he was "saying his office." Some priests referred to the book affectionately as "my wife," but for others the office was so lengthy and sometimes so obscure in its Latin translation of the Psalms that it was a duty, a real chore, an obligation that had to be fulfilled even when that meant fighting to stay awake as the midnight hour approached. Only on very rare occasions would priests ever pray the office together, and even more rare would be the attendance of lay people, perhaps at Sunday Vespers or "Tenebrae" services during Holy Week.

With the reform of the breviary effected in the Liturgy of the Hours the Church hopes for a renewal of a more traditional approach to its official prayer, an approach which characterized the early Christians who "continued steadfastly in the teaching of the apostles and in the communion of the breaking of the bread and in the prayers" (Acts 2:42). That approach is summed up in one word, celebration.

A Joyful Experience

Celebration implies a number of things. First is a joyful experience. You cannot imagine a family celebrating the tragic, premature, death of the oldest son, killed in a violent automobile accident. And yet as Christians we celebrate the death of Jesus Christ. We are happy about it because the death of Jesus Christ was neither tragic nor premature. Rather it was the fulfillment of his purpose in becoming a man and won the victory over sin and death in resurrection. His victory was for us, and stands as our greatest assurance of God's love. In all forms of prayer we are called to celebrate this death and resurrection of Jesus Christ which has made us the holy people of God. In the words of Sunday Preface I:

> Through his cross and resurrection he freed us from sin and death and called us to the glory that made us a chosen race, a royal priesthood, a holy nation, a people set apart.

We will not always feel an exuberance during liturgical prayer, but in faith we should rouse ourselves to see how blessed a people we are, a people who should rejoice to give praise and thanks to God. It is a duty, but a joyful one, to worship God in prayer of every kind.

Prayer in Common

Secondly, celebration is something you never do alone. Think of a person far from home, family, and friends on his birthday. Feeling lost in a strange city, he eats dinner all by himself in a cafeteria. Such can hardly be considered a celebration. Celebrations are always festive, and that necessarily includes people—as we say, the more the merrier. The Church wishes that we pray its official prayer with other people, for we are saved not as individuals but precisely as members of a community, the Church, the family of God (Dogmatic Constitution on the Church, 9). Perhaps it is only on occasion that we can achieve the ideal of celebrating the Liturgy of the Hours with others, but we should not on that account neglect either prayer or the spirit of celebration. As G. K. Chesterton once observed, "Anything worth doing, is worth doing poorly." Praying the hours alone is not as good as praying with others, but it is still worth doing. And even when we are physically alone we are united through

Christ with all of our brothers and sisters throughout the world as well as with those in purgatory and heaven. United with others physically or only in spirit, we can *celebrate* the Liturgy of the Hours.

The Liturgical "Now"

Thirdly, celebration has a technical meaning which refers to the fact that we praise and thank God for a current event, for a happening in which we are included, and not merely for some saving action of God in the past. God transcends time and in liturgical celebrations he draws us, in a sense, into his eternal "now" whereby we are made contemporaries of his loving actions in salvation history. Such is the liturgical tradition not only of the Church but of Israel. Consider closely but one example from the Old Testament, a passage from Deuteronomy (5:1-3) in which the author, writing long after the event described, draws the people personally into the action of God:

> Moses summoned all Israel and said to them, "Hear, O Israel, the statutes and decrees which I proclaim in your hearing this day, that you may learn them and take care to observe them. The Lord, our God, made a covenant with us at Horeb; not with our fathers did he make this covenant, but with us, all of us who are alive here this day."

The Church continued the understanding that in the liturgy God uses his almighty power to give a current reality to the events of salvation history. Pope St. Leo the Great, who died in 461, reflected the early tradition of the Church when he said in a Christmas sermon: "All the things which Jesus did for us in his humble state belong to the past; nevertheless, today's feast renews for us the blessed coming of Jesus, born of the Virgin Mary" (Sixth Christmas Sermon). Centuries later another Pope, Pius XII, wrote: "The liturgical year devotedly fostered and accompanied by the Church is not a cold and lifeless representation of the events of the past, or a simple and bare record of a former age. It is rather Christ himself who is ever living in his Church. His mysteries are ever present and active . . ." (Mediator Dei, 165). The Second Vatican Council, in the Constitution on the Liturgy (102), confirmed this doctrine:

> Within the cycle of the year the Church unfolds the whole mystery of Christ, from the incarnation and birth until the ascension, the day of Pentecost, and the expectation of blessed hope and of the coming of the Lord. Recalling thus the mystery of redemption, the Church opens to the faithful the riches of the Lord's powers and merits, so that these are in some way made present for all time, and the faithful are enabled to lay hold upon them and become filled with saving grace.

In the prayer of the Liturgy of the Hours we should strive to have a sense, not of looking to the past, but of seeing that God is to be praised here and now because we share here and now in his saving actions of all time.

Union with Christ

Celebration implies a joyful, community experience of God's love for us. There is a fourth meaning of celebration, a meaning which underlies the previous three. Celebration includes a very active faith that we are praying, not alone or in our own name, but in union with Jesus Christ. The Constitution on the Liturgy (7) teaches us that "Christ is present when the Church prays and sings, for he promised, 'Where two or three are gathered together in my name, there am I in the midst of them.'" Drawn by the Spirit into oneness with Jesus Christ our prayer is directed through Jesus Christ to our Father in heaven.

God the Father looks down upon us and sees in us the person of his Son in whom he is well pleased. And God the Father is pleased with us as we *celebrate* the Liturgy of the Hours in union with Christ as a joyful, community experience of God's love for us.

Chapter 3

PRIVATE PRAYER AND THE LITURGY

"Pray to the Father in secret . . ." (Matthew 6:16).

In the era of liturgical renewal which prepared for Vatican II, a few enthusiasts proclaimed that all one needed for a good prayer life was the Mass and the Divine Office. Other devotions were judged to be superfluous, and liturgical prayer was considered to be entirely sufficient by itself. Not so, however, for two priests whose story made the clerical rounds about twenty years ago. The two, mindful of the occupation of some of the apostles, were spending their day off fishing. Since the fish were not biting, they had both settled back to say the breviary when a sudden squall came up and threatened to capsize the boat. One of the priests, reaching for the oars, yelled in panic to the other, "Put away that book and start praying."

Although this anecdote is lacking in any real humor, it does tend to illustrate that liturgical prayer does not meet every kind of human need, nor is it intended to do so. Liturgical prayer is community prayer and is meant to be a generous, outgoing, largely other-centered type of prayer. As community prayer it cannot possibly cater to the taste of each individual; as other-centered prayer it cannot always satisfy genuine personal needs. For a proper relationship with God we need both liturgical and private prayer, each in its own time and place.

Both Are Needed

It would seem that insufficient instruction has been given the faithful in some quarters on the need we all have for both forms of prayer. One still hears some people complain, "I don't like the new Mass; I can't pray

22

anymore." What this reflects is that previously they said personal, private prayers during Mass. Now with the return to the vernacular and active participation, they find no opportunity during the celebration of the Eucharist for personal devotions and intentions—an opportunity which must be found outside the Liturgy. Liturgical prayer and private prayer are both necessary, and the one cannot supply for the other. Without liturgical prayer there is usually little growth and maturity and insufficient sensitivity to the community nature of the Church. Without private prayer there is usually little opportunity for personal self-expression. Conscientious parents provide activities for the entire family as a group, but they also make opportunities for communication with each child individually. God our Father welcomes us into his home, the church, as his family, but he also invites each one of us to communicate with him individually in private.

Private Prayer Prepares

One vital aspect of private prayer is that it prepares for liturgical prayer. In the liturgy the primary orientation is to the Father through the Son in the unity of the Holy Spirit. Liturgical prayer is trinitarian, not in the sense that it will develop a "devotion" to each of three persons, but in the sense that it comes alive only in the awareness of our relationships to the persons of the Trinity. We are children of the Father, not of the Son or the Holy Spirit, and liturgical prayer is eminently the prayer of the Father's children. But this prayer is liturgical (and real) only and solely in union with Jesus Christ. He is the one who makes prayer liturgical, as we pray together with him. As others have already observed, the liturgy is not looking at the person of Jesus Christ, but it is standing side by side with him and looking in the same direction as he, to the Father. And we are brought into union with Christ and moved to prayer through him by the loving force of the Holy Spirit, who makes us one in him. The liturgy presumes that we have an understanding and appreciation of the place of the Son and the Holy Spirit in our prayer to the Father. It is within private prayer and meditation that we develop this understanding and appreciation.

The Son Made Flesh

In baptism and confirmation we become conformed to the image of the Son. Our true identity is realized to the extent that we live out this initial conformity and celebrate it in the liturgy. To become truly ourselves, chil**dren of the Father, we must become another—Jesus** Christ, the only Son of the Father. But first we must know the Son of the Father in whose image we are made. This image is not an abstraction. The Son has become flesh in Jesus Christ, someone we can come to know and identify with, someone who is human like us in all things but sin.

One aspect of private prayer should be a meditation on the humanity of Jesus Christ. In reflective reading of the gospels we can come to know Christ Jesus in his varied human states as the early Christian communities of the four evangelists knew him. Reflections on the mysteries of Jesus Christ within the prayerful atmosphere of the rosary can also develop a warm intimacy with him. A sense of closeness and warmth with any person depends on how well we know the person, but usually in our human experience we become closest to a person when we share with him his time of crisis or sorrow. Personal prayer, then, should include loving reflection on the passion narratives of the gospels, the praying of the sorrowful mysteries of the rosary, and the making of the stations of the cross. We must reflect on the entire mystery of Christ from his incarnation and birth through his resurrection and ascension, but the likelihood is that we will draw closest to Jesus Christ through attention to him in his time of crisis.

The Holy Spirit

Love is a driving force, and the Holy Spirit is that force in the life of Jesus, moving him ever toward the Father. To fulfill our destiny we must be open to the Spirit. Most of us desperately need time for peace and quiet to allow the Spirit to work within us. The average American adult ingests between ten and twenty thousand words a day in newspapers and magazines. He listens to the radio for about seventy-five minutes a day. He is awakened by a clock radio, tunes in while driving his car, and falls asleep at night as an automatic switch turns off the radio next to his bed. In addition he spends several hours each day watching television, more on the weekends. Battered as we are by almost ceaseless noise and distraction we need to de-stimulate our senses to lessen the constant flow of sound and images into a weary brain. We must not be afraid of silence, as we force ourselves to turn off the radio, the stereo, the television, and put down our newspapers and magazines—at least during some time of the day. We don't have to play the radio every time we get into the car. We don't have to have the TV on all evening. But we do have to search for solitude to think and to pray. In quiet we can extend the invitation, "Come, Holy Spirit."

Liturgical Flavor

In order to catch the flavor of the trinitarian orientation of the liturgy, I can think of nothing better than a regular.and reflective reading of the magnificent hymn found in Ephesians 1:3-14. This passage reveals why Jesus taught us to pray "Our Father," how we are one with Christ as children of the Father, and in what way the Spirit enters our lives. Another excellent passage is the entire eighth chapter of Romans. We should "take to heart these words and think of them at home and abroad, whether we are busy or at rest."

Progress in prayer can be derived from a diligent reading of the gospel according to Luke. It is very much a gospel of prayer: in it we hear Jesus present an extensive teaching on prayer and we witness his example of prayer. We also meet other prayerful people, particularly Mary, Zechariah, and Simeon, for it is from this gospel that the Church has taken its major canticles in the Liturgy of the Hours: the Magnificat at Vespers, the Benedictus at Lauds, and the Nunc Dimittis at Compline. Try reading Luke's gospel all in one sitting. It is an unsually revealing and rewarding experience.

Time with God

Celebrating the Mass and the Liturgy of the Hours daily together with additional attention to private prayer places a great demand on a person and absorbs a considerable portion of his day. Is so much time necessary? Is it really practical? What good does it actually accomplish? Is it, in short, worth it? These may be good questions in any context, but don't dare ask them of two people who are in love concerning the time they spend with each other. When people are in love, being together is an end in itself. And if we could be open to the movement of the Spirit, the Spirit of love, we would cherish moments spent in prayer and we would yearn to have more time to spend with God. We would begin to live here on earth the life of our eternal destiny. Filled with the Holy Spirit and balanced by him between quietism and activism, our love for God would overflow into our love for others. Our days and our entire lives would indeed be made holy.

Chapter 4
KNOWING THE PSALMS

"The Spirit himself pleads for us . . ." (Romans 8:36).

Progress in praying the Liturgy of the Hours depends to some extent on a study of the Psalms. Such study need not be scholarly or academic, and one should not hesitate to consult a commentary for fear that it will be too deep or complicated. Many readable commentaries are available in English today, each of which has its own special merits. Only a few simple guidelines will be mentioned here.

There are several approaches to the study of the Psalms. Perhaps the best and most current is that which considers the Psalms according to literary types. In English literature poems can be classified as lyrics, dramas, narratives, or epics. Such classifications are not exhaustive and one poem may overlap two or more categories. In biblical literature the Psalms can be classified as hymns of praise and thanksgiving, prayers of trust and lament, royal psalms, wisdom psalms, and salvation history psalms. Such classifications are not exhaustive (some authors, for instance, add to the list "liturgical psalms" and "songs of Zion"), and one psalm may overlap two or more categories. The advantage of determining the literary type is that a person praying the Psalm feels more at home with the prayer, senses a context, and can thereby enter into the meaning and spirit of the prayer with greater confidence. The average person who does not consider himself a scripture scholar and has never had a course in the Psalms will be delightfully surprised at how easy it usually is to recognize the type.

Praise and Thanksgiving

A little over one-fourth of all the Psalms are hymns of praise and thanksgiving. Although not the most numerous of the types, the songs of praise and thanksgiving are the heart of the Psalter and from them flows a life that influences the other Psalms. They sing of God's wisdom and power as Creator, his loving guidance and salvation of his people, and his other favors. For examples see the final Psalm of Morning Prayer for any day. Further comments on this type will be made in Chapter Six.

Lament and Trust

About sixty Psalms can be classified as prayers of lament or complaint, and nine as prayers of trust. The Psalms of lament are the most "human" of the Psalms, and one schooled in a puritanical spirituality may be shocked by their bluntness and directness. Without apology or hesitation the psalmist demands at times that God rouse himself and do something about the ills and injustices he or the community is enduring. Consider the insistent tone of Psalm 13 as found in Daytime Prayer for I Tuesday:

> How long, O Lord, will you forget me?
> How long will you hide your face? . . .
> Look at me, answer me, Lord my God!

We should not be reluctant to pray these Psalms with all their demands upon God. Remember that the approach is inspired by God himself. Moreover, such demands manifest a belief in God's power and a trust in his goodness. A further consideration of this type of Psalm will be given in Chapters Five and Six.

Other Types

Royal psalms (eight in number) flow from experiences in the life of a king in Israel, but as prayed by the Church in the light of fuller revelation they are applied to Christ the King. See for example Psalm 2 (Office of Readings for I Sunday) and Psalm 110 (Evening Prayer for Sunday II). The wisdom psalms are basically meditations in the presence of God on the meaning of life and its problems. The very first Psalm belongs to this type (see Office of Readings for I Sunday). A lengthy but excellent example of this type is Psalm 37 (Office of Readings for II Tuesday). (Incidentally, this last Psalm is also acrostic, that is, its structure in Hebrew is determined by a pattern in which the initial letters of the verses follow the sequence of the alphabet, a poetic technique in Hebrew which is totally lost in translation with the result that we may find acrostic psalms lacking in any apparent organization. Only eight Psalms use the acrostic device.) Salvation history psalms are poetic summaries of God's saving actions in the history of his people. The Fourth Eucharistic Prayer shares in the style and spirit of these Psalms. For a beautiful example, see Psalm 105 (Office of Readings for I Saturday, B).

Human and Divine

Naturally much more can and should be said about the Psalms, as the great number of commentaries attests, but more cannot be said within the limits of this work. Two points, however, are most important to keep in mind about the Psalms. The first is that they are human compositions which have sprung from human experiences. They are the prayer of men and women who, though far removed from us in time and culture, are like us in our humanity with all of our strength and weakness, our faith and wonderment, our happiness and our sorrow. In their humanness the Psalms transcend eras and cultures. They belong to us as well as to our forebears in faith. The second point is that the Psalms are divine compositions. Like all of scripture, they are the word of God in the words of men. Seeing these prayers as given us by God himself, we can enter into them without hesitation, knowing that they are the right way to pray.

As St. Athanasius observed, "the Psalms have a unique value in that most of scripture speaks *to* us, whereas the Psalms speak *for* us."

Chapter 5

APOSTOLIC PRAYING OF THE PSALMS

"Pray for all men" (1 Timothy 2:1).

Priests who have been around a while have seen a lot of changes in the Divine Office over the past generation: abbreviations, revisions, translations, rearrangements, and even new names for the book. But through all the developments in our time and during past ages in the Office, one thing remains constant: the Psalms are the heart of the Church's prayer book. They are a form of prayer eminently suited to the person who would love God and his neighbor as Jesus has loved us.

God and Neighbor

The Psalms are manifestly God-centered; in fact, one hundred and thirty-three of them mention God by name in the very first verse. Their obvious God-centeredness makes them supremely appropriate for those who by baptism have become conformed to the image of Jesus Christ who directed his whole life to the Father.

And yet the Psalms can also be termed apostolic, especially as they are used by the Church in the Liturgy of the Hours. The Hours are the public prayer of the Church, offered not only in the name of the Church but also for the Church. "For the Church" means for people—real, live people, not some abstraction. As we go through the Psalms we discover almost every possible human emotion. We may not be able to identify in every instance with these emotions, but they do reflect the condition and the state of mind of those for whom we are praying. Perhaps a large number of these people rarely, or possibly never, think to turn to God in prayer as their feelings range from elation to despair. My suggestion is that we attempt to pray not only for these people, but in their very person.

In the Person of Others

Let me give some examples of what I mean. In Psalm 71 I find this sentiment: "O God, you have taught me from my youth and I proclaim your wonders still. Now that I am old and grey-headed, do not forsake me, God." I don't think of myself as old and I have only a tinge of gray, but I can picture elderly men and women almost forgotten in a rest home, enveloped with a lethargy which precludes much inclination to pray. When I turn to Psalm 71 during Daytime Prayer on III Monday, I pray in the person of these elderly people.

Consider Psalm 86. As I pray this Psalm during Monday Night Prayer I find the following complaint: "I am poor and needy. . . . The proud have risen against me; ruthless men seek my life." If I have had a good day on Monday, these words do not fit my mood. And yet I know that there are many people in the world for whom Monday is indeed blue, even bleak, as they feel abandoned by relatives and ignored by friends, left alone to struggle through life. In their person I can pray to God: "Turn and take pity on me. O give your strength to your servant."

Numerous are the Psalms which sing the praises of God for all his blessings. Who knows how many people have received favors from God without a thought of praising and thanking him? I can pray in their persons. And so with people who need to seek God's forgiveness for sins, his help in temptation, and his comfort in sorrow. Of course I should as much as possible make the sentiments of the Psalms my own and I should unite myself with those who do remember to pray, but there seems to be a particular urgency about praying in the person of people who either ignore, or simply forget about, God.

A Valuable Reality

The idea of praying in the person of others is not mere sentiment or bad poetry. It represents a reality. We are all one in the body of Christ, united by his headship of both the entire human race and the Church. Jesus Christ himself is the link which binds us all to one another. Liturgical prayer is offered in union with Jesus Christ, and in this prayer the oneness we have with others becomes a living, dynamic inter-action. St. Paul reminds us that all the members of the body of Christ are to be concerned for one another. He then goes on to say: "If one member suffers, all the members suffer with it; if one member is honored, all the members share its joy. You, then, are the body of Christ. Every one of you is a member of it" (1 Corinthians 12:25ff).

Pray we must for others if we are to be a people of faith. It is easy enough for one sincerely to adopt the attitude that he is too busy working for the good of others to pray for them or in their person or whatever. But such an attitude comes perilously close to a sense of self-sufficiency which is far removed from the dispositions of the poor in spirit, the *Anawim,* who know that all depends on God. It is indeed far removed from the spirit of Jesus himself who, in the midst of people's needs and demands, made time to spend whole nights in prayer. The effort we make to pray in the person of others is a measure of our faith.

Praying in the name of others is also an unselfish apostolate. If I visit the elderly in a rest home, I will probably find at least one person with a sparkle of gratitude in his eyes. The person who comes to me to unburden himself and discovers a listener will at the end say something like, "I feel much better now. Thanks a lot." It is heartwarming to experience the appreciation of another who has been helped, but in apostolic prayer

I am reaching out to the unseen member of the body of Christ, the unknown person in great need. There is no response of gratitude. Apostolic prayer is indeed an unselfish act of love.

Of course prayer can be an excuse for inactivity in the apostolate, an inappropriate substitute for zeal, a cover-up for laziness. Such a condition is inexcusable and cannot be justified by an appeal to the importance of prayer. But it does seem that most good people are tempted to go in the opposite direction, to replace prayer with activity and to think that doing is more important than praying. A proper perspective can be gained by remembering these words of Jesus Christ: "I am the vine, you are the branches. He who lives in me, and I in him, will produce abundantly, for apart from me you can do nothing. . . . If you live in me, and my words stay part of you, you may ask what you will, it will be done for you" (John 15:5 and 7).

In the Liturgy of the Hours the Church commends to us the Psalms as both a God-centered and a truly apostolic form of prayer.

PART II
THE HOURS

Chapter 6
MORNING PRAYER

"My mouth shall declare your praise" (Psalm 51:17).

The sanctification of the day begins with Morning Prayer. This prayer should be said as the first of the day, as soon after rising as reasonable. Its theme is expressed in the old Latin term, *Lauds,* for it is principally a prayer of praise. Many of us have had the practice from youth of making our morning prayer a plea for help during the day as well a consecration or offering of the day to God. But the Church's emphasis is a little different. In our first waking moments and perhaps with eyes still filled with sleep, we are urged to look to heaven and to acknowledge that God is God and therefore worthy of our praise and thanks.

Setting the Theme

The theme is set by the opening words of the entire day's office as we make a small sign of the cross on our lips and say, "Lord, open my lips and my mouth will proclaim your praise." This theme is highlighted in the final psalm which, according to an ancient practice of the Church, is always a hymn of praise. It is the keynote psalm and deserves special attention. Frequently the very first word of this final psalm is "praise," as in II Sunday: "Praise God in his holy place . . ." (Psalm 150). Or the word "praise" appears early in the Psalm, even in the first verse as on I Sunday: "Sing a new song to the Lord, his praise in the assembly of the faithful. . . ." (Psalm 149). Some important synonyms in the Psalms for praise are "glory" (I Monday, Psalm 29), "bless" (I Friday, Psalm 100), and most importantly "thanks" or "thanksgiving" (III Monday, Psalm 96). In a sense all the Psalms are songs of praise, but the twenty-three different Psalms selected as the final ones for Morning Prayer present a special emphasis on praise as their theme.

The Meaning of Praise

It is very difficult to define praise. Essentially it is an appreciation of God, a recognition of him in his goodness. It is looking toward heaven and saying, "Lord, you alone are God, living and true." Perhaps best, praise is the expression of love for someone who is God.

Some authors like to make a distinction between praise as a consideration of God in himself and thanksgiving as a consideration of God in relation to us. The distinction is specious. The Scriptures and the Liturgy simply do not look upon God in himself. Although it is true that the human mind can come to a knowledge of God in himself by the light of reason, the God of revelation makes himself known through his actions in salvation history. Christians, enlightened by both Old and New Testament revelations, look to heaven and say, "Father, we acknowledge your greatness; all your actions show your wisdom and love" (Fourth Eucharistic Prayer). We come to know God, and therefore to see that he is worthy of praise, through his loving actions toward us.

In thinking about the meaning of praise, it is helpful to reflect on the word "eucharist." It is a Greek word which means "to give thanks." As the Church has traditionally used it, this word has a deeper meaning than simply a response of gratitude for a favor received. It reflects a usage of the Jews who did not really have an expression which was the exact equivalent of our word, "thanksgiving." Among the Jews "to give thanks to God" meant to praise and glorify him, to bless his name. Such is the meaning of *benedixit* in the Latin formula of the consecration, which is rendered quite correctly in English as "he gave you thanks and praise." While we must be grateful for personal favors granted us by God, we should learn to see that even small gifts are a sign of God's goodness which is worthy of our praise.

Recall the story of the ten lepers in Luke's gospel (17: 11-19). The one leper who wanted to show his thanks "came back *praising* God in a loud voice." Jesus himself interpreted that praise as a form of thanksgiving: "Was there no one to return and give thanks to God except this foreigner?" Consequently in our new liturgical translations two words are often joined: thanks and praise. At the beginning of the preface, for instance, when the priest says, "Let us give thanks to the Lord our God," the people respond, "It is right to give him thanks and praise." Indeed it is right to give thanks and praise to God. That is why the Church puts before us the theme of praise as our first prayer of the day.

The Opening Psalm

According to the General Instruction on the Liturgy of the Hours, the first Psalm is chosen because of its suitability for the morning. Only rarely, however, is there a reference in these Psalms to the time of day, as in Psalm 57 for I Thursday: "Awake, my soul, awake, lyre and harp, I will awake the dawn." Of the twenty-eight possibilities for this initial Psalm over four weeks, fourteen, or half, of the selections are prayers of lament. Scholars admit that the term, "lament," is not entirely satisfactory. The word connotes a bleak, pessimistic view of life, but such is not the mood of these Psalms. They turn to God in times of human distress with the firm belief that he alone has the means to lift a person out of the depths of human needs. As such they are prayers of praise to God for his loving power. The spirit of the prayers of lament is summed up in Psalm 42:

> Why are you cast down, my soul,
> why groan within me?
> Hope in God; I will praise him still,
> my savior and my God.

The Psalms of lament place us in the human predicament as the waking day begins. They immediately call to mind how much both we and others need God, and are well suited to be prayed in an apostolic spirit (see Chapter Five). The other choices for the first Psalm are varied hymns and songs of praise and thanksgiving in accord with the Church's idea of what Morning Prayer should be.

Old Testament Theme

Between the two Psalms of Morning Prayer we find an Old Testament canticle. These canticles are hymns to God drawn from books of the Bible other than that of the Psalms. (While one can enter into the prayers of these canticles without elaborate study, some knowledge of the context is helpful; it is beyond the scope of this book, however, to go into that background, which can easily be uncovered in any good commentary on the Old Testament.) The use of these canticles is based on the fact that the early morning hour suggests the theme of Old Testament salvation history. At the beginning of the day we celebrate the beginnings of God's plan. God's providential movements in history are important to us in the Christian era. As Pope Pius XI pointed out, we are all spiritually Semites; Abraham is our father in faith. The coming of Christ is a fulfillment of the covenant made with Abraham, and the entire Old Testament is a salvific action of God which reaches its climax in the person of Jesus Christ. Nor are God's actions buried in the past. We are united with the chosen of the Old Testament as the one people of God and share with them God's loving kindness toward them. Christians should identify with the "we," the "our," and the "us" in the following verses from Psalm 126:

> When the Lord delivered Zion from bondage,
> it seemed like a dream.
> Then was *our* mouth filled with laughter,
> on *our* lips there were songs.
> The heathens themselves said: "What marvels
> the Lord worked for them!"
> What marvels the Lord worked for *us!*
> Indeed *we* are glad.

God is one and the same in the Old and the New Testament eras. The God of Israel is the God of Christians:

> O Lord, you have been our refuge
> from one generation to the next.
> Before the mountains were born
> or the earth or the world brought forth,
> you are God, without beginning or end (Psalm 90).

The Old Testament theme reaches both its high point and its perspective in the canticle of Zechariah (the *Benedictus*) which is used in every Morning Prayer. The name, "Zechariah," literally means "God has remembered," and is symbolic of God's keeping his promises made in the Old Testament. This hymn resounds with Old Testament allusions: David, the prophets, Abraham, the covenant. God is indeed to be blessed and praised because he has remembered all his promises to his people, promises of which the Baptist, son of Zechariah, is the last prophet in a long line of outstanding men raised up by God to carry his plan forward to the day of Christ.

Perspective: The Resurrection

The Church does not celebrate Old Testament themes as if Christ has not yet come or as if Christ has not yet died and been raised to the glory of God the Father. Zechariah's canticle helps give perspective to Old Testament themes. Zechariah's canticle is, it must be remembered, a *gospel* canticle (that is why it is prayed standing and why the sign of the cross is made as it begins). The Church has long seen in the dawn a symbol of the resurrection of Christ, and this daily canticle, drawing on the symbolism of dawn, lifts us in an instant to the realization of Christ's glorious victory, as with the sun a brilliant illumination floods the world:

> In the tender compassion of our God
> the dawn from on high shall break upon us,
> to shine on those who dwell in darkness and the
> shadow of death,
> and to guide our feet into the way of peace.

The fullness of the Christian theme is expressed in the conclusion of the final prayer: "We ask this through our Lord Jesus Christ, your Son, who lives and reigns with you and the Holy Spirit, one God, for ever and ever."

Consecration of the Day

While the Church obviously intends that we begin our day with the praise of God, it does not entirely neglect the popular orientation toward a prayer for help during the day. Following the canticle of Zechariah, the Church gives us a series of invocations whose primary purpose is to consecrate the day to God. These petitions lead to the Church's first of three official daily prayings of the "Our Father" (the other two are at Mass and Evening Prayer). Morning Prayer concludes with a collect type prayer such as that found at Mass.

Preserving the Spirit of Morning Prayer

Every effort should be made to celebrate Morning Prayer as the first prayer of the day. Before we undertake any work or other human activity we should present ourselves to God in the spirit of Psalm 5:

It is you whom I invoke, O Lord.
In the morning you hear me;
in the morning I offer you my prayer,
watching and waiting.

Even an early morning Mass ideally should be preceded by Morning Prayer, and it is worth the effort to rise a little earlier for the sake of this prayer. Although the General Instruction allows for a combining of Morning Prayer with Mass, it seems better to keep the two distinct. The reason is that they have entirely different purposes. Morning Prayer sanctifies the first moments of the day, whereas Mass is the culmination of the entire day no matter when it is celebrated.

The Church has never apologized for its predilection for the praise of God, nor need it do so now in a busy, task-oriented world. We are made to sing the praises of God for all eternity and that destiny begins here on this earth. God has no need of our praise, it is true, and our prayer adds nothing to his greatness; rather we are the ones who grow to fulfillment through a life of praise (cf. Preface for Weekdays IV). God is good to predestine us to praise his glory, to be conformed to the image of his Son whose entire life was a priestly life of praise of his Father. This praise should have, as it did for Jesus, all the tender affection of a child for a good father. Our praise is the expression of love for someone who is God.

Happy and holy is the day which begins with the Church's Morning Prayer of praise.

Chapter 7
DAYTIME PRAYER

"Thy will be done" (Matthew 6:10).

Following the example of the apostolic Church, early Christians were accustomed to pray several times a day in the midst of their work. Monastically these varied times evolved into the hours known as Terce (about 9:00 a.m.), Sext (about noon) and None (about 3:00 p.m.). The Second Vatican Council directed that those obliged to office in choir were to continue to celebrate these hours, but that for others one of the hours would be sufficient. The reduction to one hour is a recognition of the modern problem of living in a busy world, but the Church has retained one of these hours so that we may follow the ancient tradition of praying during the day while occupied with our work.

God's Will

"Daytime Prayer" is the name usually given now to the one hour retained by the Church from among the original three. It is designed to be prayed not precisely at noon (Sext), but at some reasonable time which spans the gap from Morning Prayer to Evening Prayer. Somewhere between 11:00 a.m. and 1:00 p.m. would seem to be about the ideal, but an earlier hour (approximating Terce) or a later hour (approximating None) is suitable.

The theme of this prayer is God's will. Its purpose is to recall to our minds that whatever our work may be, we are committed to following God's will in imitation of Jesus who became obedient even to death on a cross (Philippians 2:8). It also serves as a way of consecrating ourselves anew to the words we pray at Mass as well as at Morning and Evening Prayer, "Thy will be done." Since the Eucharist is our celebration of that obedience

of Christ which won his exaltation from the Father
(Philippians 2:9), Daytime Prayer has a special relationship to the Eucharist. It can look back to a morning
Eucharist as a reaffirmation of our dedication to God's
will as expressed in the Mass, or it can look forward to
and prepare for an evening Eucharist.

Theme Psalm

The theme of this prayer is set by the first Psalm
which is taken from Psalm 119 (with the exception of
Sundays, First Monday, and Third Friday; we will see
why later). Psalm 119 is the longest Psalm in the entire
Psalter, running for 176 verses. It is divided into sections
of eight verses over the weekdays of four weeks. It has
but one topic throughout: God's will. The Psalmist men-
tions God's will in every one of the 176 verses without
exception, and in order to avoid repeating the same word
he uses many synonyms, such as commands, statutes,
precepts, words, promises, etc. It is important to see
that these expressions are indeed but synonyms for
God's will lest we interpret this Psalm in some legalistic
sense. Notice the italicized words in the following section
of the Psalm as used on III Tuesday:

> Lord, how I love your *law!*
> It is ever in my mind.
> Your *command* makes me wiser than my foes;
> for it is mine for ever.
> I have more insight than all who teach me
> for I ponder your *will.*
> I have more understanding than the old
> for I keep your *precepts.*
> I turn my feet from evil paths
> to obey your *word.*
> I have not turned away from your *decrees;*
> you yourself have taught me.
> Your *promise* is sweeter to my taste
> than honey in the mouth.

I gain understanding from your *precepts;*
I hate the ways of falsehood.

The second and third Psalms are chosen from among those not used in the other hours, but more often than not they are suited to being prayed with an apostolic spirit in the manner described in Chapter Five. As apostolic prayers these Psalms are eminently appropriate for Daytime Prayer.

Exceptions to Psalm 119

The first Psalm of Daytime Prayer on First Monday is not 119 but 19. Its theme is the same as that of Psalm 119, God's will. On Third Friday Psalm 22 is used in three sections. It is the Psalm placed on the lips of the dying Jesus by St. Matthew, "My God, my God, why have you forsaken me?" (Matthew 27:46), and is used because of the relationship of every Friday to Good Friday. Sunday Daytime Prayer contains Psalms suited to the celebration of the Lord's Day. First and Third Sundays employ Psalm 118 in three parts. This Psalm is a beautiful song of thanksgiving to God for his saving power. The New Testament sees this Psalm as fulfilled in Christ (Matthew 21:24 and Acts 4:11), and the Church has incorporated verse 24 ("This day was made by the Lord; we rejoice and are glad") into its Easter celebration of which every Sunday is a reflection. Second and Fourth Sundays begin Daytime Prayer with Psalm 23 (the Good Shepherd) and divide Psalm 76 into two parts for the second and third psalms. Psalm 76 is a hymn of praise of God for his protecting presence among his people.

Reading and Prayer

Following the psalmody Daytime Prayer presents a brief reading from scripture. The purpose of this reading is to keep the Church's perspective that prayer is always dialogue: we speak to God and God speaks to us. The hour is concluded with a prayer which on ferial days and memorials is related directly to the time of day; on feasts and solemnities the prayer is proper.

A Practical Prayer

Daytime Prayer is very practical and even necessary in our busy world as it calls us back to a realization that all our occupations should be the carrying out of God's will. The fact that it is often difficult or troublesome to pray this hour is itself an indication of how vital the hour is to help us keep a prayerful realization of what we are about in our lives. The person who makes up his mind that this prayer is important will take the means to say it daily. When we find that we will be away from home at the time this prayer should be said, we can take the book with us and make the opportunity to set aside the five minutes needed for a devout praying of this hour. A priest, for example, who is busy with visiting the sick and perhaps has an appointment at the chancery can sit in his car in a parking lot and say this prayer. A layman at work can set aside five minutes during his lunch break. Those living in community may find Daytime Prayer an appropriate way to begin or end a noon meal together. Where there is a will, there is indeed a way.

Union with Jesus and Mary

Daytime Prayer as emphasizing the will of God in our lives helps bring us into contact with two great moments in New Testament salvation history, its beginning and its climax. When the angel announced to Mary that she was to be the mother of Jesus, she responded to God's invitation by saying, "Be it done to me according to your word" (Luke 1:38). At that moment Jesus the Savior took flesh in the womb of Mary. St. Thomas Aquinas, following St. Luke's presentation of Mary as the personification of the Church, points out that Mary gave consent in the name of us all. This consent we can affirm in Daytime Prayer. When Jesus was about to enter upon those final events of his salvific life, he struggled to accept the will of his Father during his prayer in the garden, as he pleaded "Father, if it is your will, take this cup from me." Then in a moment of supreme loving obedience, he cried out, "Yet not my will but yours be done" (Luke 22:42). "For the sake of the joy which lay before him he endured the cross, heedless of shame" (Hebrews 12:2). "And it was thus that he humbled himself, obediently accepting even death, death on a cross! Because of this God highly exalted him and bestowed on him the name above every other name" (Philippians 2: 8f). Daytime Prayer helps to unite us with Jesus in his prayer, "Not my will but yours be done," and directs us toward that moment of exaltation by the Father when we will be worthy of the name Christian.

The busier we are the more we need this simple but meaningful prayer given to us by the Church through the guidance of the Holy Spirit who helps us in our weakness to pray as we ought in order to make holy the day.

Chapter 8
EVENING PRAYER

"My soul proclaims the greatness of the Lord"
(Luke 1:46).

The proper time for Evening Prayer, or Vespers, is the very late afternoon or early evening when the day is drawing to a close. To capture the spirit of Evening Prayer is not easy in our busy modern world. For earlier generations the hours of darkness meant rest from work, quiet relaxation, a time to sit peacefully and read or simply reflect, but in our times the day is often far from over with the coming of evening. The anxieties and tensions of the working hours intrude upon the evening with little respect for our instinctive yearning for peace and calm. Effort will be needed not only to set aside time for Vespers but also to wash from our mind the preoccupations and worries of the day so that we may spend precious moments with God in celebration of his loving kindness manifested in the person and mission of Jesus Christ.

The Theme of Fullness

The hour for Vespers, when the day is at its full, sets the theme. As Morning Prayer is a celebration of Old Testament revelation leading to Christ, so Evening Prayer is a celebration of the fullness of revelation. Every Vespers is situated in that "supper hour" when Jesus, having loved his own who were in the world, showed the depth of his love (John 13:1).

Each Evening Prayer is composed of two Psalms and a New Testament Canticle. Twelve of the Psalms selected are royal psalms, commemorating some event which has its setting in the experience of a king. These kingly Psalms as prayed by the Church are understood in the light of further revelation which brings the person of Christ the King into sharper focus as the fulfillment of kingship in Israel. Other Vesper Psalms are the Great Hallel Psalms (120-136), which include the Gradual Psalms. The latter (Psalms 120-125) are probably the prayer of pilgrims as they went up to Jerusalem for the great feasts of Israel. The Hallel group formed a part of the celebration of the Passover Supper and there is good reason to believe that Jesus prayed these Psalms with his apostles at the Last Supper. The entire collection is most appropriate for the hour of Evening Prayer. The remaining selections are "easy" and popular Psalms which most people can enter into with little difficulty.

In the Canticle following the Psalms the Church has restored to liturgical use beautiful hymns from the New Testament, some of which had their source in the early worship of the Christian communities while others quickly became a part of liturgical celebrations. These Canticles, taken from Colossians, Ephesians, Philippians, 1 Peter, and Revelation, heighten the New Testament theme of Evening Prayer.

The Magnificat

The New Testament theme reaches its climax in the gospel Canticle popularly known as "The Magnificat." This simple but splendid Canticle is a mosaic of Old Testament texts, a meditation on the goodness of God and his saving deeds of loving kindness toward his people throughout history which reach their fullness in the person of Jesus Christ. From this meditation flows a joyful, even jubilant, spirit of praise and thanksgiving: "My soul proclaims the greatness of the Lord; my spirit rejoices in God my savior."

Luke places the words of this Canticle on the lips of Mary not merely as she is an individual or even precisely as she is the mother of the Savior. In the full Lucan context Mary is the personification of the Church and its model in prayer. Following the lead of St. Luke, the Vatican Council declared: "Mary is hailed as the pre-eminent and altogether singular member of the Church and as the Church's model and excellent exemplar in faith and charity" (Constitution on the Church, 53). Consequently as we pray this Canticle we should realize that with Mary we as members of the Church are the lowly servant whom God has lifted up. The Almighty has done great things for *us,* and has mercy on *us* who fear him. And so we proclaim the greatness of the Lord and rejoice in God our Savior.

Intercessory Prayers

The concluding prayers of Vespers are different from those of Lauds. The invocations at Lauds consecrate or commend the day to God. The intercessions at Vespers are intended to be prayers for the benefit of the whole world. As such they are a generous kind of prayer and reflect an expansive spirit which reaches out in love and concern for everyone without exception. These intercessions are prayed in union with Jesus Christ who "opened his arms on the cross" to embrace all of mankind. They express the "catholic" aspect of Christian prayer and fulfill the exhortation of the Apostle: "I urge that petitions, prayers, intercessions and thanksgiving be offered for all men, especially for kings and those in authority, that we may be able to lead undisturbed and tranquil lives in perfect piety and dignity. Prayer of this kind is good, and God our Savior is pleased with it, for he wants all men to be saved and come to know the truth" (1 Timothy 2:1-4).

Spontaneous prayers are appropriate following the formulated intercessions, but such prayers should reflect a universal concern. For example, one may be mindful of a relative who is to be operated on; his prayer could possibly be phrased in this way: "For my brother who is to undergo surgery tomorrow and for all those who are seriously ill, we pray to you, Lord."

The Spirit of Evening Prayer

The Eucharist should ordinarily be separated from Evening Prayer. If the Eucharist is celebrated before the dinner hour, Evening Prayer can easily follow dinner, or vice versa. It is not ideal to combine the two since they have different purposes. If the Eucharist must follow Evening Prayer immediately, one concession seems in order: that the intercessions be omitted from Evening Prayer in favor of the Prayer of the Faithful at Mass.

Evening Prayer sanctifies the closing hours of the day. It is the Church's way of living out the words of Psalm 141: "Let my prayer arise before you like incense, the raising of my hands like an evening oblation." Although all the hours are ideally prayed in common, a special effort should be made to pray Vespers in common since this hour most clearly reflects in its New Testament theme the nature of the Church as the new people of God. Each one of us should wish to join with his spiritual brothers and sisters in Christ to sing the praises of God who so loved the world that in the fullness of time he sent us his only-begotten Son.

Chapter 9
THE OFFICE OF READINGS

"Speak, Lord, your servant is listening"
(1 Samuel 3:9).

The Office of Readings, formerly known as Matins, has a long history with origins in the vigil service of the early Christians. Before the end of the first century it had become the practice for Christians to spend the entire night of Easter in prayer and meditation upon the scriptures, waiting until the dawn of the resurrection. Later an abbreviated form of vigil preceded every Sunday as little Easter. This night-time service with concentration on readings from scripture was the forerunner of that part of the office which came to be known as Matins.

In the fourth century monasticism spread rapidly and the monks enthusiastically embraced the customary prayers of Christians as their supreme obligation. By the time of St. Benedict, who died around the year 543, this largely scriptural service had become a daily office consisting of three divisions, called nocturns, to be prayed through the night. Because of its length and the time of its celebration Matins became the office of monks to the exclusion of the laity and even the rest of the clergy.

The Second Vatican Council wished to restore Matins to a form suitable for everyone. It directed that for those obliged to office in choir Matins should retain its nocturnal character and length, but that for others it should be shortened and adapted in such a way that it could be prayed at any hour of the day. As a result the Office of Readings now consists of three brief Psalms and two readings. The first reading is biblical and the second is taken from the writings of the Fathers of the Church or other authors, or from the lives of the saints.

Nature of the Office of Readings

The Office of Readings is unique among the liturgical hours, not only in that it is not related to a particular time of the day, but also in that it has its own orientation. Morning Prayer and Evening Prayer, Daytime Prayer and Night Prayer, all are primarily people speaking to God. Although in these hours the Church is very careful to maintain the dialogical aspect of prayer (man to God and God to man), listening is given little more than a nod. In the Office of Readings the reverse is true; therein the emphasis is on listening to God's word both in scripture and in other sources. "Speak, Lord, your servant is listening" sums up the spirit of the Office of Readings. This emphasis tends to establish a balance in the entire Liturgy of the Hours between speaking and listening.

The purpose of the Office of Readings is different from that of the Liturgy of the Word in the Mass. The readings during Mass are not principally didactic, but are proclaimed for the purpose of moving us to worship God in the Eucharist. By means of this purpose the Liturgy of the Word forms one act of worship with the Liturgy of the Eucharist (Constitution on the Liturgy, 56). In the Office of Readings, especially on ferial days, the lessons are an end in themselves in the sense that they are not immediately directed toward some specific goal. We should come to the Office of Readings to hear the word of God, to ponder it at leisure and as deeply as possible. We should listen to God's word in a spirit of openness, eager to allow the word to form our thinking, to shape our lives, and to lead us wherever the Spirit wills. The Office of Readings, within the span of fifteen minutes or so, is meant to take on the character of a day of recollection or mini-retreat, the Holy Spirit himself being the retreat master.

Special Offices

The Office of Readings for Solemnities, Feasts, and most Memorials is of a different nature from that for ferial days. On these occasions the Office of Readings is thematic and usually carries the theme of the liturgical observance more completely than do the other hours. As such it forms an excellent preparation for a eucharistic celebration by enlightening us concerning the meaning of the liturgical observance. It is still permissible to anticipate the Office of Readings after Vespers of the preceding day, and such anticipation before a Solemnity or Feast can be beneficial, especially if there is to be an early morning Eucharist. (For ferial days such anticipation seems to have no real value.) When the Eucharist is celebrated later in the day, anticipation is not necessary since the Office of Readings can easily be prayed before the Eucharist. On the other hand, some may prefer to have the Office of Readings after the Eucharist as a way of reflecting back upon its celebration and prolonging its spirit.

The special or "proper" Office of Readings helps to develop within us a spirituality which is formed by the liturgy of the Church in both its seasonal and sanctoral cycle. This is a solid spirituality, drawn not from merely human ideas or motives, but from the life of Jesus Christ and the example of the saints.

Other Uses

The Office of Readings can also be used to enhance days of recollection, retreats, and other devotions. On days other than Solemnities and Feasts it is quite correct to select Psalms and readings in accord with some specific theme or purpose which would ordinarily be covered in a conference or sermon. A homily may follow the Readings as part of the Office. This arrangement has the advantage of placing a topic within the context of prayer. Devotions in honor of Mary or the saints can also be well served by being molded into the structure of an Office of Readings.

Reflective Listening

Since the emphasis in every form of the Office of Readings is on listening, rushing through it will accomplish little. This Office should be prayed at a time and in circumstances suitable for reflection. In common, a considerable period should be given to silence after the Readings even before the responsories are made. The Church has been very careful to construct the Office of Readings in such a way that it may be prayed at any hour of the day precisely so that it may be prayed with an openness to hear the word of God.

Chapter 10
NIGHT PRAYER

"Into your hands I commend my spirit" (Ps 31:6).

Night Prayer or Compline is to be prayed as the last prayer of the day just before retiring, even after midnight if necessary. This prayer often becomes the favorite of many people, possibly because its symbolism is so clearly beautiful and forceful. Darkness and sleep are biblical and poetic symbols of death. Night Prayer prepares us not only for sleep but also for death. It is the Night Prayer of the day and of life itself.

Elements of Night Prayer

The prayer is preceded by an examination of conscience since symbolically we are about to appear before God in death. The pause should be of some length to allow time for sincere reflection. (This is the "official" time for an examination of conscience; the pause at the beginning of Mass is for reflection on our unworthiness, an acknowledgment of sinfulness, but not an examination of conscience.) The silent examination should include a personal expression of contrition and amendment.

The Psalms of Night Prayer are of two kind, prayers of trust and of lament. They are the sentiments of people who rely totally on God (the Psalms of trust) or who through their human predicaments come to realize that in God alone can man place complete confidence (the Psalms of lament). Trust and confidence are most appropriate themes of Night Prayer, because there is something awesome and fearful about both sleep and death. For primitive man sleep meant that he exposed himself to dangers from the elements, the animals, and his human enemies. In sleep he was defenseless, and there was no guarantee that he would wake to see the dawn. Perhaps the fear of primitive man is at least dimly reflected in little children who hate to go to bed. To some extent they "don't want to miss anything," but within them there is a fear of darkness and sleep. As the parent turns out the light, a little child says, "I want a drink of water." He could have had a gallon of water before going to bed and he would still ask for a drink. He isn't thirsty. He is afraid and is looking for some tactic which will keep his parent in the room a little longer.

With the sophistication of adulthood we lose our fear of sleep. And yet we have no guarantee that the "mechanism" which wakes us will work. Nor do we have any sure knowledge that we will wake from the sleep of death, that awesome passage into the unknown. But we do have faith. We have faith that God will awaken us from the sleep of death. We have confidence and trust that through death we will share in the life of the resurrected Christ. How appropriate for Night Prayer, then, are the Psalms of confidence and trust.

Dying and Rising with Christ

The theme of confidence and trust reaches a climax in the responsory to the scripture reading: "Into your hands, Lord, I commend my spirit." These words of Psalm 31 St. Luke placed on the lips of the dying Savior (Luke 23:46). Through these same words we can effectively unite our death with that of Christ. And because of our union with him, we can say with complete serenity, "You have redeemed us, Lord God of truth." In the gospel Canticle of Simeon, which follows the responsory, we identify with an old man who is about to die, a man who approaches death willingly because he has seen salvation in the person of Jesus Christ.

By a long tradition dating back at least to St. Benedict, who died around the year 543, the final prayer of the day concludes with a hymn to our Lady. Several choices are available, two of which have explicit allusions to death; in the "Hail, Holy Queen," we say: "After this our exile show to us the blessed fruit of your womb, Jesus," and in the "Hail Mary" we say: "Pray for us sinners now and at the hour of our death." But with any of the hymns to our Lady we should realize that we are honoring the glorified mother of the Savior, that blessed woman who in her assumption has already shared in the resurrection of Christ. Mary, the model of the Church, taken body and soul to heaven, is a sign that we as members of the Church will pass through death to a sharing in the resurrection of Christ.

Importance of This Hour

Night Prayer centers on the paschal mystery, the heart of Christianity. We become Christians by sharing in the paschal mystery, the death and rising of Christ, through baptism. We celebrate this mystery in the Eucharist. We live it every day since every day is like a little lifetime, the paschal mystery in miniature, as in sleep we die and in waking come to life again. At a time chosen by God this cycle will end when we make the last passage through physical death to the fullness of life. In death we have our final, physical sharing in the death of Christ and we look to the life-giving hand of the Father who will raise us to the glory of Christ's resurrection.

Our weariness at the end of the day can make Night Prayer a chore. It is so easy simply to fall into bed without a further thought that we may be tempted to forget all about still another prayer. But our fatigue itself should remind us that we are frail, that every moment brings us closer to the ultimate moment of death. We need to place ourselves in the hands of our loving Father before we close our eyes in sleep just as we hope to be received by our Father when we close our eyes in death.

Night Prayer sanctifies the final hour of the day. But it does more. It sanctifies our entire life since Christian living centers on the paschal mystery. Dying is the most important act of living. It is the final expression of faith in God the Father as life-giver. As such death should be embraced willingly, and in the sentiments of Night Prayer we make our death voluntary in union with that of Christ. Truly this prayer is the Night Prayer of the day and of life itself.

SUMMARY

"By your gift I will utter praise in the vast assembly" (Psalm 22:26).

1. Because of its emphasis on the Psalms, the Liturgy of the Hours is different from ways of praying which were formative for most of us in our early impressions. As inspired prayers the Psalms are of unique value and we go to them and to the entire Liturgy not to find favorite prayers but to be formed according to the movement of the Spirit.

2. In union with Christ the celebration of the Liturgy of the Hours is a joyful, communal experience of God's ever-present love for us.

3. The Liturgy is not intended to exhaust one's prayer life or to substitute for private prayer. In fact, private prayer is quite necessary, especially as a preparation for liturgical prayer.

4. A knowledge of the Psalms contributes to a more prayerful attitude in their use, but such knowledge need not be esoteric. The Psalms are both human and divine.

5. The "humanity" of the Psalms makes them appropriate as an apostolic prayer to be offered in the person of others through our mutual union in Christ.

6. In our first waking moments we are to look toward heaven and praise God for his goodness. The beginning of the day suggests the theme of the beginnings of salvation history, the Old Testament, but as seen in the light of the resurrection of Christ.

7. The principal theme of Daytime Prayer is dedication to God's will in union with Jesus Christ who because he was obedient unto death was exalted by the Father.

8. The time for Evening Prayer, when the day is at its full, sets the theme of the fullness of revelation in the New Testament. It is eminently the prayer of the Church in imitation of Mary, the type and model of the Church. Every Vespers is situated in that supper hour when Jesus, having loved his own who were in the world, showed the depth of his love.

9. The emphasis in the Office of the Readings is on a meditative listening to God's word in scripture and other sources.

10. In Night Prayer sleep is a symbol of death. The theme is complete trust and confidence: "Into your hands I commend my spirit."